I0457847

MIND-BLOWING
ANCIENT
CIVILIZATIONS

*100 Lost Worlds and Their Incredible
Secrets*

FELIX GRAYSON

MINDSPARK
PUBLISHING

CONTENTS

BEFORE WE DIVE IN...

Did you know that this is just **one** of many **mind-blowing** books waiting to be discovered?

What if I told you there's a **world of jaw-dropping, unbelievable, and downright bizarre facts** across **sports, science, history, mysteries, and more**—each one packed with stories that will **challenge what you thought you knew?**

EVER WONDERED WHAT IT'S LIKE TO...

- Witness **record-breaking Olympic moments** that defy human limits?

- Explore **real-life conspiracy theories** that sound too wild to be true?

- Discover **unsolved mysteries** that still leave experts baffled?

- Learn about **billionaires, stock market crashes, and money secrets?**

- Find out how **robots, AI, and space travel are shaping the future?**

- Experience the **most extreme sports, legendary battles, and shocking events?**

This is just the beginning. The **100 Mind-Blowing series** covers it **all.**

WANT TO SEE WHAT'S NEXT?

Go to **FelixGrayson.com** and explore the **growing collection** of books and audiobooks that will **entertain, amaze, and keep you coming back for more.**

Curiosity doesn't stop here—this is just the beginning. What will blow your mind next?

INTRODUCTION

Welcome to *100 Mind-Blowing Ancient Civilizations*, a collection designed to make you say, "Wait… how is this real?" From long-lost cities to astonishing technologies, this book is packed with stories that will make you look at ancient history in a whole new way.

Ever wondered how a civilization could build a city in the clouds—or move giant stones without modern machines? What about ancient brain surgery, desert plumbing, or entire empires that just… disappeared? These are just a few of the jaw-dropping stories waiting for you inside. Each one has been carefully chosen to surprise, fascinate, and maybe even spark a few "Wait, why didn't we learn this in school?" moments.

Whether you're a curious wanderer, a trivia buff, or someone who just loves a good mystery, this book has something for you. You can read it straight through, flip to a random page, or use it to impress your friends with wild facts from lost worlds. There's no one way to explore the past—and that's exactly what makes it so fun.

So settle in, open your mind, and get ready to

travel through time. Because the ancient world wasn't just old—it was *absolutely mind-blowing*.

Mind-Blowing Ancient Civilization #1

THE CITY BUILT ON HUMAN SKULLS

In the heart of ancient Mesoamerica, the Aztec capital of **Tenochtitlán** held a chilling secret: a massive tower made entirely of human skulls. Known as the **Huey Tzompantli**, this gruesome structure stood near the Templo Mayor and was stacked with thousands of real skulls from sacrificial victims.

For centuries, it was dismissed as myth or exaggeration—until archaeologists **actually found it** in 2015 beneath modern-day Mexico City. Over **600 skulls** have been uncovered so far, many belonging to women and children, suggesting ritual offerings were more complex than previously believed.

The tower wasn't just a symbol of power—it was a brutal message to enemies and a sacred display for the gods. Imagine walking through the bustling capital and seeing a skull wall staring back at you.

Mind-Blowing Ancient Civilization #2

CLEOPATRA WASN'T EGYPTIAN

Despite being Egypt's most famous queen, **Cleopatra VII** wasn't actually Egyptian—she was Greek! Born into the **Ptolemaic dynasty**, Cleopatra descended from **Ptolemy I**, a Macedonian general under Alexander the Great who took control of Egypt after Alexander's empire fractured.

The Ptolemies ruled Egypt for nearly 300 years, and while they adopted some Egyptian customs, they clung tightly to their Greek roots. Cleopatra was the **first in her line to actually speak Egyptian**, a savvy move that helped her win favor with her people.

So while Hollywood might picture her as a native Egyptian goddess, her ancestry, politics, and even her spoken language told a very different story—one of strategy, identity, and survival in a world where bloodlines were power.

Mind-Blowing Ancient Civilization #3

THE CITY THAT VANISHED WITHOUT A TRACE

The ancient city of **Mohenjo-Daro**, part of the **Indus Valley Civilization**, was one of the world's earliest urban centers—boasting advanced drainage systems, multi-story buildings, and even public baths—**over 4,000 years ago**.

Then, mysteriously, it all disappeared.

There are **no signs of war, no signs of famine**, and **no known explanation** for its sudden abandonment. The entire civilization—millions strong—just seemed to fade into history, leaving behind eerily well-preserved ruins and **no written records** we can understand.

To this day, archaeologists and historians still **don't know** why Mohenjo-Daro collapsed. Some suspect climate change, others point to shifting rivers. But one of the most advanced cities of the ancient world simply... vanished.

Mind-Blowing Ancient Civilization #4

THE VIKINGS BEAT COLUMBUS BY 500 YEARS

Long before Columbus "sailed the ocean blue," **Viking explorers** had already crossed the Atlantic and **settled parts of North America**.

Around the year **1000 AD**, Leif Erikson—son of Erik the Red—sailed from Greenland and established a short-lived settlement called **Vinland**, located in what is now **Newfoundland, Canada**.

For centuries, this was considered Norse legend—until archaeologists **uncovered the ruins** of a Viking village at **L'Anse aux Meadows** in the 1960s. The site contained unmistakable Norse artifacts, confirming the Vikings were the **first Europeans** to set foot in the New World—**nearly 500 years before Columbus.**

It's one of the greatest "wait, what?!" moments in history—proof that history books sometimes miss a chapter or two.

Mind-Blowing Ancient Civilization #5

THE ROMANS HAD CONCRETE THAT HEALS ITSELF

The mighty Romans built structures that have stood for **over 2,000 years**—and the secret wasn't just brilliant engineering. It was the **concrete**.

Modern scientists have discovered that **Roman concrete** had a unique ability: **it could heal its own cracks**. Made with a special mix including **volcanic ash**, this ancient recipe allowed the material to react with moisture over time and essentially "re-seal" itself.

That's why Roman aqueducts, harbors, and buildings like the **Pantheon** have survived centuries of wear and weather, while modern concrete often crumbles within decades.

Only recently have engineers started unlocking the full secrets of this lost technology—and now we're trying to copy it.

Mind-Blowing Ancient Civilization #6

THE MAYANS PREDICTED SOLAR ECLIPSES

The ancient **Maya civilization** was obsessed with the skies—and they were *really* good at reading them. Using nothing but the naked eye and handmade tools, Mayan astronomers could **accurately predict solar eclipses** centuries in advance.

They developed complex calendar systems like the **Dresden Codex**, which included eclipse tables so precise that modern astronomers have been stunned by their accuracy.

This was thousands of years before telescopes or computers—yet they tracked celestial cycles with such skill that their predictions rival ours today. And they did it while also building pyramids, running vast trade networks, and inventing chocolate.

Not bad for a so-called "lost" civilization.

Mind-Blowing Ancient Civilization #7

THE LIBRARY THAT RIVALED ALEXANDRIA

Most people know about the **Library of Alexandria**, but fewer have heard of its powerful rival: the **Library of Nineveh**, built by the Assyrian king **Ashurbanipal** in the 7th century BCE.

Located in what is now **modern-day Iraq**, this library held over **30,000 clay tablets** written in cuneiform, covering everything from astronomy to literature—including the **Epic of Gilgamesh**, the world's oldest known epic poem.

Unlike Alexandria's fragile scrolls, many of these clay tablets **survived fires, wars, and centuries underground**—giving us a direct link to ancient Mesopotamian knowledge.

When it was discovered in the 1850s, it completely changed our understanding of early civilizations. It was a time capsule, just sitting there, waiting to be read.

Mind-Blowing Ancient Civilization #8

SAMURAI WERE ALSO BUREAUCRATS

When you think of **samurai**, you probably picture sword-wielding warriors bound by honor. But during much of Japan's feudal history, especially under the **Tokugawa Shogunate**, many samurai spent more time at a **desk than on a battlefield**.

As peace settled over Japan in the 17th century, samurai were transformed into **civil administrators**, managing government records, collecting taxes, and enforcing laws.

Some even wrote poetry, studied philosophy, and became scholars. The sword was still worn, but it became more a symbol of status than survival.

So yes—some of history's most feared warriors were also some of its **most well-read pencil pushers**.

Mind-Blowing Ancient Civilization #9

THE PERSIANS INVENTED AIR CONDITIONING

Long before the modern AC unit, the **ancient Persians** were keeping cool in the desert heat—with a brilliant bit of architectural engineering known as a **windcatcher**, or **"badgir."**

These towering structures, dating back over **2,000 years**, used wind flow and evaporative cooling to **naturally lower indoor temperatures**—sometimes by more than 20 degrees Fahrenheit. They were often paired with underground water channels called **qanats**, which helped push cool air throughout homes and palaces.

The best part? No electricity. Just smart design, wind, and water. Some traditional buildings in Iran still use them today.

The ancient world wasn't just wise—it was refreshingly chill.

Mind-Blowing Ancient Civilization #10

CHINA'S ARMY OF CLAY WAS BOOBY-TRAPPED

In 1974, farmers digging a well near **Xi'an, China** uncovered one of the most jaw-dropping finds in history: the **Terracotta Army** — thousands of life-sized clay soldiers buried to guard **Emperor Qin Shi Huang** in the afterlife.

But here's the wild part: ancient texts suggest the tomb itself was protected by **booby traps**, including **crossbows rigged to fire automatically** if disturbed. And inside the emperor's unopened burial chamber? A model of his empire, complete with **rivers made of flowing mercury**.

Modern scans have detected **high levels of mercury** in the soil, suggesting the legends may be true. So far, the central tomb remains sealed — too dangerous to explore.

It's an ancient mystery wrapped in a deadly defense system.

Mind-Blowing Ancient Civilization #11

THE INCAS HAD NO WRITTEN LANGUAGE

The **Inca Empire**, one of the largest and most advanced in the Americas, built cities, highways, and suspension bridges—**all without a written language**.

Instead, they used a mysterious system called **quipu**—bundles of cords with **knots** tied in various positions and colors. These knots recorded everything from census data to taxes and possibly even stories or laws.

For centuries, quipu was dismissed as primitive bookkeeping, but recent research suggests it might have been a **full-blown information system**, perhaps even a non-verbal **written language** unlike anything else on Earth.

To this day, no one has fully cracked the quipu code—making the Inca one of the most advanced civilizations to **vanish without ever writing a word**.

Mind-Blowing Ancient Civilization #12

ANCIENT GREEKS USED A COMPUTER

In 1901, divers off the coast of **Antikythera, Greece** discovered a corroded lump of bronze from a sunken Roman shipwreck. Inside it? What turned out to be an **ancient analog computer**, now known as the **Antikythera Mechanism**.

Dating back to the **2nd century BCE**, this complex device used **gears and dials** to **predict eclipses**, track the movements of planets, and even calculate the dates of the **Olympic Games**.

Its design was so sophisticated, nothing like it appeared again for over **a thousand years**. For decades, scientists couldn't figure out how it worked—but with modern imaging, they've finally started to decode its genius.

It wasn't just gears—it was **Greek engineering light-years ahead of its time.**

Mind-Blowing Ancient Civilization #13

STONEHENGE WAS PART OF A SUPER SITE

Everyone knows **Stonehenge**, but fewer realize it was just one piece of a **massive prehistoric complex**—a kind of ancient sacred landscape filled with **hidden monuments, ritual paths**, and **buried mysteries**.

In recent years, ground-penetrating radar revealed dozens of previously unknown **structures beneath the surface**, including a ring of **huge pits** nearly 2 miles wide and remnants of wooden henges, burial mounds, and processional routes.

These discoveries suggest that Stonehenge wasn't just a standalone monument—it was part of an **enormous ceremonial network** used for centuries, possibly even millennia.

Turns out, one of the world's most famous ancient sites was just the tip of the stone iceberg.

Mind-Blowing Ancient Civilization #14

THE OLMECS MADE COLOSSAL STONE HEADS

Before the Maya, before the Aztecs—there were the **Olmecs**, one of Mesoamerica's oldest civilizations. And what they left behind still stuns archaeologists today: **colossal stone heads**, each weighing up to **40 tons** and standing over **9 feet tall**.

Carved from giant basalt boulders, these heads are believed to represent **Olmec rulers**, complete with distinctive facial features and helmet-like headgear. Some were transported **over 50 miles** from the quarry—without wheels or metal tools.

No one knows exactly how they did it. The logistics alone boggle the mind. But these monumental sculptures were created as early as **1200 BCE**—centuries before the rise of better-known Mesoamerican empires.

The Olmecs may be ancient history, but their stone stares are unforgettable.

Mind-Blowing Ancient Civilization #15

EASTER ISLAND STATUES HAVE BODIES

The giant stone heads of **Easter Island**—called **moai**—are famous worldwide. But here's what most people don't know: **they're not just heads. They have full bodies buried underground.**

Archaeologists digging around the statues discovered that many moai extend **deep below the surface**, complete with torsos, arms, and inscriptions carved into their backs.

Why were they buried? It's still debated. Some believe it was due to soil erosion over centuries; others think the statues were intentionally set into the earth as part of religious rituals.

Either way, these "heads" were never just heads—**they were massive, mysterious full-body monuments** from a civilization that left no written record of how or why they were made.

Mind-Blowing Ancient Civilization #16

THE GREAT ZIMBABWE WAS A STONE EMPIRE

In the heart of southern Africa lies the ruins of **Great Zimbabwe**, a massive stone city built entirely without mortar. Dating back to the **11th century**, it was the capital of a powerful African kingdom that controlled trade across the region.

Its stone walls—some over **30 feet tall**—still stand today, enclosing royal palaces, towers, and temples. At its height, Great Zimbabwe may have housed **up to 20,000 people** and was a hub for gold, ivory, and cattle trade with far-off lands like **China and Persia**.

For years, European colonists tried to claim that such architecture couldn't have been built by Africans. They were wrong. It was.

Great Zimbabwe is a powerful reminder of a **rich, complex African past** that refuses to be ignored.

Mind-Blowing Ancient Civilization #17

THE HITTITES MASTERED IRON FIRST

Long before iron changed the course of history, one ancient civilization had already figured it out: the **Hittites**.

Around **1500 BCE**, the Hittites of Anatolia (modern-day Turkey) became the **first known culture to smelt and work iron**, giving them a massive edge in weapons and tools. While the rest of the world still relied on bronze, the Hittites quietly entered the **Iron Age centuries ahead of schedule**.

Their methods were so advanced—and so secret—that when their empire collapsed, it **delayed the spread of ironworking** across the ancient world by hundreds of years.

It wasn't just technology. It was an arms race... and the Hittites were way ahead.

Mind-Blowing Ancient Civilization #18

THE NAZCA LINES CAN ONLY BE SEEN FROM ABOVE

Etched into the dry plains of southern Peru are the **Nazca Lines**—massive geoglyphs stretching **hundreds of feet across**, depicting animals, plants, and abstract shapes. But here's the kicker: **they're nearly impossible to see from the ground.**

Created over **1,500 years ago**, these intricate designs were made by removing reddish surface stones to reveal lighter earth underneath. The lines have remained astonishingly well-preserved thanks to the region's dry, windless climate.

The big mystery? The Nazca had **no way to fly**, yet the shapes only make sense from **high above**. Some believe they were ritual pathways, others think they were astronomical calendars. Alien theories? Plenty.

Whatever their purpose, one thing's certain: **the desert was their canvas, and the sky was their audience.**

Mind-Blowing Ancient Civilization #19

ANCIENT INDIA HAD PLASTIC SURGERY

Over 2,000 years ago, **ancient Indian physicians** were performing surgical procedures that would make even modern doctors blink—**including plastic surgery**.

The legendary surgeon **Sushruta**, often called the "father of surgery," described detailed techniques for **rhinoplasty** (nose reconstruction) in his text, the **Sushruta Samhita**, written around the 6th century BCE. His methods involved using skin flaps from the cheek or forehead to rebuild noses—**a technique still used today**.

He also covered **eye surgeries, hernia repairs, and even caesarean sections**—long before anesthesia or antiseptics existed.

While Europe was still centuries away from catching up, ancient India was already rewriting the surgical playbook.

Mind-Blowing Ancient Civilization #20

THE SAHARA WAS ONCE GREEN AND WET

It's hard to imagine today, but the **Sahara Desert**—now the largest hot desert in the world—was once a lush, green paradise.

Between **10,000 and 5,000 years ago**, during a period known as the **African Humid Period**, the Sahara was covered in **grasslands, lakes, and even forests**. Cave paintings found deep in the desert depict **elephants, hippos, and people swimming**—clear signs of a thriving, wetter world.

This dramatic climate shift likely forced early human populations to **migrate**, helping spread agriculture and culture across Africa and into the Middle East.

The desert we know today was once a cradle of life—and might be again one day, depending on the planet's next move.

Mind-Blowing Ancient Civilization #21

SPARTANS HAD A SECRET POLICE

While ancient Sparta is often glorified for its fearless warriors, there was a **darker side** to its society—one ruled by fear and surveillance.

Enter the **Krypteia**: a **secret police force** made up of young Spartan men sent out at night to **spy on and even assassinate** members of the **helot** population—the enslaved majority who did all the farming and manual labor.

These missions weren't just tolerated—they were **state-sponsored tests** of stealth, loyalty, and brutality. The Krypteia operated in shadows to keep the helots in check, ensuring they never rose up against their Spartan overlords.

So behind the legend of noble warriors was a chilling system of **covert control and fear-based dominance.**

Mind-Blowing Ancient Civilization #22

MESOPOTAMIANS INVENTED THE FIRST RECIPES

Long before Michelin stars and food blogs, the ancient **Mesopotamians** were writing down **actual recipes**—and they're the **oldest known in the world**.

Clay tablets dating back to around **1700 BCE** from the city of **Babylon** detail instructions for preparing elaborate dishes like stews made with **meat, vegetables, garlic, and spices**. These weren't survival rations—they were gourmet meals, served at royal banquets.

Some recipes even included **timing, ingredients, and steps**, making them the ancient ancestors of modern cookbooks. And yes—**chefs today have tried recreating them**.

Turns out, the cradle of civilization was also the **cradle of cuisine**.

Mind-Blowing Ancient Civilization #23

THE PHOENICIANS CREATED THE ALPHABET

While many ancient cultures wrote in complex symbols or pictographs, it was the **Phoenicians** who revolutionized writing by creating the **first true alphabet**.

Developed around **1050 BCE**, their system used **22 letters**—all consonants—and could be combined to form countless words. It was **simple, flexible, and easy to learn**, making writing more accessible than ever before.

The Greek, Latin, Hebrew, and Arabic alphabets all evolved from this **Phoenician script**, meaning the letters you're reading **right now** are descended from an ancient trading civilization on the Mediterranean coast.

In short? Every time you write, you're using **Phoenician tech**.

Mind-Blowing Ancient Civilization #24

THE MINOANS HAD FLUSH TOILETS

Long before Rome's famous aqueducts, the **Minoan civilization** on the island of **Crete** had already mastered something incredibly modern: **indoor plumbing**—including **flushable toilets.**

Dating back to around **2000 BCE**, the Minoans built palaces like **Knossos** with multi-level buildings, drainage systems, and ceramic pipes that carried waste and water. One particular royal bathroom even featured a **toilet with a water-flushing system**, centuries before the rest of the world caught up.

They also had **bathtubs, sinks, and sewage control**, all designed with remarkable engineering and an eye for comfort.

Basically, while other civilizations were still figuring out where to go—the Minoans were already flushing in style.

Mind-Blowing Ancient Civilization #25

THE CELTS BUILT HILLFORT CITIES

Long before castles dotted Europe, the **Celts** were building massive **hillforts**—fortified cities perched high on ridges, often with **earthen ramparts**, **timber walls**, and commanding views of the surrounding land.

These structures weren't just for defense. Many, like **Danebury** in England or **Oppidum of Manching** in Germany, served as **bustling centers of trade, religion, and governance**, complete with workshops, granaries, and marketplaces.

Some hillforts housed **thousands of people**, making them among the largest pre-Roman urban centers in Europe.

Forget the stereotype of wild tribes in forests— **the Celts were organized, innovative, and fiercely sophisticated.**

Mind-Blowing Ancient Civilization #26

THE FIRST BRAIN SURGERY WAS IN PREHISTORY

Long before hospitals or anesthesia, ancient humans were performing **brain surgery**—and many patients **actually survived**.

Archaeologists have found **skulls from as far back as 7,000 years ago** with carefully carved holes—evidence of a procedure known as **trepanation**, where part of the skull was removed, possibly to relieve pressure or treat head trauma.

Even more shocking? Many of these skulls show signs of **bone regrowth**, meaning the patients **lived for months or even years** after the operation.

From Peru to Siberia, trepanned skulls have been discovered across the globe, proving that ancient civilizations were far more **medically daring** than we give them credit for.

Mind-Blowing Ancient Civilization #27

THE ETRUSCANS TAUGHT ROME HOW TO BE ROME

Before Rome became an empire, it was a **scrappy little city-state**—and it learned much of its culture, architecture, and religion from a mysterious neighbor: the **Etruscans**.

Living in what is now **central Italy**, the Etruscans were master builders, metalworkers, and traders. They gave the Romans everything from **gladiatorial games** to **arched architecture**, and even the symbols of Roman kingship—like the **fasces**, later used by emperors.

Their influence was so deep that many early Roman gods were **Etruscan imports** with new names.

Though eventually absorbed by Rome, the Etruscans helped shape the very foundation of one of history's greatest civilizations—and most people have never even heard of them.

Mind-Blowing Ancient Civilization #28

THE KHMER EMPIRE BUILT A MEGA-CITY

Most people know **Angkor Wat** as a stunning temple—but few realize it was just one part of an **enormous ancient metropolis**.

At its peak in the 12th century, the **Khmer Empire** built **Angkor**, a sprawling city in modern-day Cambodia that may have been **the largest urban center in the world** at the time, housing **up to a million people**.

Recent lidar scans through the jungle have revealed vast networks of **roads, canals, reservoirs, and suburbs,** hidden beneath the vegetation for centuries. It was a **hydraulic civilization**, using advanced water management to thrive in a monsoon climate.

It wasn't just temples—it was a megacity **centuries ahead of its time**, swallowed by the jungle and only now being rediscovered.

Mind-Blowing Ancient Civilization #29

THE ARABS PRESERVED GREEK KNOWLEDGE

During Europe's **Dark Ages**, when much classical knowledge was being lost, **Muslim scholars** in the Islamic Golden Age were **translating, preserving, and expanding** the works of ancient Greece and Rome.

In cities like **Baghdad**, especially at the famed **House of Wisdom**, scientists and philosophers translated texts by **Aristotle, Plato, Galen, and Ptolemy** into Arabic—and didn't stop there. They **improved upon** the math, astronomy, medicine, and philosophy they inherited.

Without this movement, many foundational texts might have **disappeared forever**—and the Renaissance may never have happened.

So, the next time you solve for "x" or gaze at the stars, thank the scholars who kept ancient knowledge burning bright through the dark.

Mind-Blowing Ancient Civilization #30

THE ANDES HAD A 25,000-MILE ROAD SYSTEM

The **Inca Empire** didn't have the wheel, horses (until Europeans arrived), or a written language—but they still built one of the most **impressive transportation networks** in history.

Known as the **Qhapaq Ñan**, this road system stretched over **25,000 miles** through the Andes, connecting mountain peaks, valleys, deserts, and jungles across six modern countries. Some paths were so high they reached **over 16,000 feet in elevation**.

Bridges made of woven grass, rest stations called **tambos**, and runners known as **chasquis** allowed messages and goods to move rapidly across the empire—**faster than many parts of Europe at the time**.

All of it, engineered without iron tools or beasts of burden. Just **stone, muscle, and genius.**

Mind-Blowing Ancient Civilization #31

SOCRATES NEVER WROTE ANYTHING DOWN

One of the most famous philosophers in history, **Socrates**, left behind exactly **zero written works**. Not a single scroll, tablet, or scrap of parchment.

Everything we know about him comes from the writings of **his students**, especially **Plato**, who used Socrates as the main character in many of his philosophical dialogues. It's through these accounts that Socrates' ideas—like the **Socratic method**, ethical reasoning, and critical questioning—have echoed through time.

But here's the kicker: we don't actually know how much of it was **Socrates himself**, and how much was **Plato's interpretation**.

So one of the most influential thinkers in Western history remains a **mystery wrapped in someone else's words**.

Mind-Blowing Ancient Civilization #32

THE HUNS USED SCALPELS ON SKULLS

The fearsome **Huns**, who terrorized the Roman Empire in the 4th and 5th centuries, weren't just brutal warriors—they also practiced a strange and advanced form of **cranial surgery**.

Archaeologists have uncovered Hunnic skulls with signs of **trepanation**, where precise holes were cut into the cranium—possibly to treat injuries, relieve pressure, or even for ritual purposes. These weren't sloppy wounds from battle—they were **deliberate, careful procedures**, and some skulls show clear signs of **healing**, meaning patients **survived**.

It's a chilling but fascinating glimpse into a culture usually only seen through the lens of conquest.

Turns out, the Huns knew how to crack heads in more ways than one.

Mind-Blowing Ancient Civilization #33

THE YORUBA HAD A CALENDAR OLDER THAN EUROPE'S

The **Yoruba people** of West Africa developed a complex and precise **calendar system** that may be **older than the Gregorian calendar** used today.

Rooted in astronomical observation and spiritual cycles, the Yoruba calendar is based on a **four-day week**, a **seven-week month**, and a **364-day year**, closely tied to the movements of the moon and stars. It also includes intricate **divination systems** like **Ifá**, which use mathematical patterns to interpret fate and guide decisions.

Some scholars trace its structure back **over 10,000 years**, making it one of the **oldest surviving timekeeping systems** on Earth.

So while Europe was still counting with sundials, the Yoruba were already **charting cosmic rhythms with mathematical precision**.

Mind-Blowing Ancient Civilization #34

THE ASSYRIANS INVENTED THE FIRST LIBRARIES

Long before the concept of public libraries took root, the ancient **Assyrians** were already **archiving knowledge** for future generations.

In the 7th century BCE, King **Ashurbanipal**—the same ruler behind the Library of Nineveh—created what is considered the **first systematically organized library** in history. It contained over **30,000 clay tablets**, sorted by subject and tagged with **cataloging systems**, including phrases like *"for future kings."*

These tablets included everything from myths and medicine to math and military strategy, written in **cuneiform**.

It wasn't just a collection—it was **an information hub**, centuries before Dewey decimal systems or digital archives.

Ashurbanipal didn't just want to rule his empire—he wanted to **archive it.**

Mind-Blowing Ancient Civilization #35

ANCIENT PERUVIANS BRED SUPER-SPUDS

Long before potatoes became a global staple, the **ancient civilizations of the Andes**, like the **Chavín** and later the **Inca**, had already domesticated **hundreds of potato varieties**—many of which were adapted to thrive in extreme mountain climates.

These early agriculturalists developed techniques to grow potatoes at high altitudes, in freezing temperatures, and in poor soil. They even invented a freeze-dried potato preservation method called **chuño**, which allowed the food to last **for years**—perfect for long-term storage or military campaigns.

Modern geneticists now realize that the biodiversity of today's potatoes owes **everything** to this ancient ingenuity.

Turns out, the spud wasn't just a side dish—it was a **technological triumph**.

Mind-Blowing Ancient Civilization #36

THE MOUND BUILDERS SHAPED NORTH AMERICA

Long before skyscrapers and stadiums, the **ancient Mound Builder cultures** of North America were raising massive earthworks that still boggle the mind.

From around **1000 BCE to 1500 CE**, civilizations like the **Adena, Hopewell**, and **Mississippian** built enormous mounds—some for burials, others for ceremonies, astronomy, or elite residences. The most famous, **Cahokia**, near modern-day St. Louis, had a population **larger than London** at the time and featured a central mound taller than a 10-story building.

These structures required **millions of hand-carried baskets of earth**, precise planning, and deep social organization—yet their builders left **no written records**.

These weren't simple piles of dirt—they were the beating heart of ancient American cities.

Mind-Blowing Ancient Civilization #37

THE FIRST PEACE TREATY WAS EGYPTIAN

While ancient civilizations were often at war, one of the earliest examples of **diplomatic peace** comes from **ancient Egypt and the Hittites**—two powerful empires that clashed in the famous **Battle of Kadesh** around **1274 BCE**.

After years of bloody conflict, Pharaoh **Ramses II** and Hittite King **Hattusili III** signed what is considered the **world's first known peace treaty**. The agreement promised mutual aid, prisoner exchanges, and a royal marriage alliance.

Copies of the treaty survive in both **hieroglyphs** and **Akkadian cuneiform**, and a replica even hangs today **at the United Nations Headquarters** in New York as a symbol of early diplomacy.

It proves that even in ancient times, **words could win where weapons failed**.

Mind-Blowing Ancient Civilization #38

THE AKSUMITES MINTED THEIR OWN COINS

While many ancient African empires traded in gold dust or goods, the **Kingdom of Aksum**—located in what is now **Ethiopia and Eritrea**—was one of the few sub-Saharan civilizations to **mint its own coins.**

As early as the **3rd century CE**, Aksumite kings issued **gold, silver, and bronze coins** with inscriptions in Greek and later Ge'ez, the local script. These coins were used for international trade with **Rome, India, and Arabia**, proving that Aksum was a **global player** in the ancient economy.

Even more impressive? Some coins depicted **Christian symbols**, making Aksum one of the first states in the world to feature Christianity on its currency—**before many parts of Europe.**

This was no fringe kingdom. Aksum was **rich, connected, and cosmopolitan.**

Mind-Blowing Ancient Civilization #39

BABYLON HAD THE WORLD'S FIRST LEGAL CODE

Long before modern laws and courtrooms, the ancient city of **Babylon** produced the **Code of Hammurabi**—one of the **earliest known sets of written laws**, dating back to around **1754 BCE**.

Commissioned by King **Hammurabi**, this towering basalt stele outlined **282 laws** covering everything from contracts and wages to criminal punishment and family disputes. It even introduced the principle of **"an eye for an eye."**

What made it revolutionary wasn't just the rules—it was that the laws were **publicly displayed**, making justice a matter of **record, not rumor**.

It was more than stone. It was a symbol of order, fairness, and the rise of a structured society.

Mind-Blowing Ancient Civilization #40

THE SOGDIANS WERE SILK ROAD SUPERSTARS

Tucked between powerful empires, the **Sogdians** of Central Asia built their legacy not through war or conquest—but through **trade, language, and diplomacy**.

From around the **4th to 10th centuries** CE, these skilled merchants dominated the **Silk Road**, acting as cultural and economic go-betweens for **China, Persia, India, and Rome**. They didn't just move silk—they carried **religions, languages, ideas, and art** across thousands of miles.

They developed their own written script, maintained multi-lingual networks, and even influenced Chinese culture—some Sogdians rose to high positions in Chinese courts!

Though few know their name today, the Sogdians were the **invisible hands shaping the ancient global economy**.

Mind-Blowing Ancient Civilization #41

THE HAURI BUILT WITH VOLCANIC CONCRETE

In the Ethiopian highlands, the ancient **Hauri civilization**—sometimes linked with early **Aksumite** cultures—crafted monumental architecture using an unexpected material: **volcanic ash.**

They developed a kind of **volcanic concrete**, similar in durability to what the Romans used, to build their **multi-story stone structures** and underground tombs. This mix hardened over time, resisting erosion and earthquakes, and allowed for precise cuts and decorative carvings.

Some of these structures, including pillar tombs and stelae, have lasted for over **1,500 years**—despite weather, time, and minimal restoration.

It's a forgotten reminder that **brilliant engineering wasn't just a Mediterranean thing**—it was happening across ancient Africa, too.

Mind-Blowing Ancient Civilization #42

THE INDUS HAD STANDARDIZED WEIGHTS

The **Indus Valley Civilization**, one of the oldest urban cultures on Earth, wasn't just advanced in city planning—they were obsessed with **precision and standardization**.

Archaeologists have uncovered **carefully calibrated stone weights** and **measuring tools** used for trade, construction, and taxation. These weights were so uniform across distant cities like **Harappa** and **Mohenjo-Daro** that scholars believe the civilization had **a centralized authority enforcing standards**—a huge achievement for the time.

Even their bricks followed a **mathematical ratio** of 1:2:4, used consistently for centuries.

In an age when most of the world was still tribal, the Indus people had already mastered **quality control and organized bureaucracy**.

Mind-Blowing Ancient Civilization #43

THE GREEKS HAD A VENDING MACHINE

Yep, the ancient **Greeks** invented the **world's first vending machine**—over 2,000 years ago.

Around the 1st century CE, engineer and mathematician **Hero of Alexandria** designed a device that dispensed **holy water** when a coin was inserted. The coin would fall onto a pan attached to a lever; the weight would open a valve and let the water flow—until the coin slipped off and the valve closed.

It wasn't just clever—it was **automated, coin-operated tech** in a time when most people didn't even have plumbing.

Hero also designed wind-powered machines, automatic doors, and even a primitive steam engine. The man was **basically the da Vinci of the ancient world.**

Mind-Blowing Ancient Civilization #44

THE NUBIANS RULED EGYPT AS PHARAOHS

When people picture ancient Egypt's pharaohs, they usually think of native Egyptians—but for nearly a century, the empire was ruled by **Nubian kings** from the south.

In the 8th century BCE, the **Kingdom of Kush**—located in modern-day Sudan—conquered Egypt and established the **25th Dynasty**, known as the **Black Pharaohs**. These rulers restored old temples, revived traditional Egyptian art, and even expanded the empire.

Far from being foreign invaders, the Nubians saw themselves as **guardians of Egyptian culture**, and they ruled with a deep reverence for its traditions.

Yet this powerful chapter in Egypt's history was often overlooked—until modern archaeology and scholarship helped bring their legacy back into the light.

Mind-Blowing Ancient Civilization #45

THE HOHOKAM BUILT DESERT CANALS

In what is now **Arizona**, the ancient **Hohokam civilization** engineered one of the most sophisticated **irrigation systems** in pre-Columbian North America—**right in the middle of the Sonoran Desert.**

Over a thousand years ago, the Hohokam carved out **over 500 miles of canals**, using only stone tools and manual labor. These canals diverted water from the **Salt and Gila Rivers** to irrigate fields of corn, beans, squash, and cotton—sustaining large, complex communities in one of the harshest environments on Earth.

Their waterworks were so advanced that **modern engineers used their layouts** as blueprints for Phoenix's early canal system.

Desert dwellers? Sure. But more importantly, **they were master hydrologists.**

Mind-Blowing Ancient Civilization #46

THE CHINESE MADE EARTHQUAKE DETECTORS

Over 1,800 years ago, during the **Han Dynasty**, Chinese inventor **Zhang Heng** created the world's **first known seismoscope**—a device that could **detect earthquakes hundreds of miles away.**

It looked like a bronze vase surrounded by dragon heads, each holding a metal ball. When seismic waves hit, the mechanism inside would trigger **one dragon to drop its ball into a corresponding frog's mouth**, pointing to the direction of the quake—even if the tremor wasn't felt locally.

Modern scientists tested replicas and found it could actually work.

Long before Richter scales, ancient China was already **listening to the rumble of the Earth**—with dragons.

Mind-Blowing Ancient Civilization #47

THE MAORI NAVIGATED WITHOUT MAPS

Long before compasses or GPS, the **Maori and their Polynesian ancestors** were **master navigators**, sailing vast distances across the Pacific Ocean with stunning accuracy.

Using **star charts memorized in their minds**, along with cues from **ocean swells, cloud patterns, bird flight paths**, and even the color of the water, these seafarers navigated thousands of miles in **double-hulled canoes**—reaching islands like **New Zealand, Hawaii, and Easter Island** centuries before European explorers.

They didn't just travel—they **settled** and **thrived**, carrying plants, animals, and entire cultures with them across an ocean bigger than any continent.

They were, quite literally, **the astronauts of the ancient seas.**

Mind-Blowing Ancient Civilization #48

THE ZAPOTECS INVENTED A WRITTEN LANGUAGE

Before the rise of the Maya or the Aztecs, the **Zapotec civilization** of ancient Oaxaca, Mexico, developed one of the **earliest known writing systems** in the Americas—**over 2,500 years ago**.

Their script, found on monuments at sites like **Monte Albán**, included symbols that represented **syllables and words**, etched into stone to record **dynasties, rituals, and conquests**. This makes it one of the **first examples of true writing** in the Western Hemisphere.

Though not fully deciphered, it's clear the Zapotecs used their writing to **document history**—not just tell myths.

Before the Maya made it famous, the written word was already **carving its mark in Mesoamerica**.

Mind-Blowing Ancient Civilization #49

THE LYCIANS INVENTED DEMOCRATIC VOTING

Before Athens got all the credit for inventing democracy, the **Lycians**—an ancient people of what's now **southwestern Turkey**—were already experimenting with **representative government**.

As early as the **5th century BCE**, the **Lycian League** united over **two dozen city-states**, each sending delegates to a central assembly based on their city's size. It wasn't just symbolic—these delegates voted on **military, legal, and economic matters**, and decisions bound the whole league.

In fact, the **U.S. Founding Fathers** admired the Lycian system—**James Madison** even cited it while crafting the U.S. Constitution.

Long before ballots and bureaucrats, the Lycians were already testing the **power of the people.**

Mind-Blowing Ancient Civilization #50

THE CHACHAPOYA BUILT CLOUD CITIES

High in the misty mountains of northern Peru, the **Chachapoya civilization**—known as the "Cloud People"—built **stone cities and fortresses** on sheer cliffs thousands of feet above sea level.

Their most famous site, **Kuelap**, rivals Machu Picchu in scale and complexity. It includes massive **stone walls, round houses**, and a stunning location that earned it the nickname **"The Machu Picchu of the North."**

They lived in constant contact with clouds, creating one of the **highest-altitude civilizations** in the Americas. And yet, much about them remains a mystery—even their language is lost.

They were warriors, builders, and sky-dwellers who turned mountaintops into **homes among the heavens.**

Mind-Blowing Ancient Civilization #51

THE SUMERIANS INVENTED THE FIRST SCHOOLS

In ancient **Sumer**, over 4,000 years ago, children—mostly boys from elite families—attended institutions called **"edubbas"**, which were essentially the **world's first formal schools**.

There, students learned to read and write **cuneiform** on clay tablets, along with math, accounting, and religious texts. Teachers didn't hold back—strict discipline, repetition, and memorization were the norm.

Why so serious? Because scribes were **essential to society**, managing everything from taxes and trade to prayers and laws.

These early classrooms gave birth to the very idea of education as a **structured system**—long before school bells and backpacks.

Mind-Blowing Ancient Civilization #52

THE EBLAITES HAD A DICTIONARY

In the ruins of **Ebla**, an ancient city in modern-day **Syria**, archaeologists uncovered thousands of clay tablets from around **2500 BCE**—and among them was what may be the **world's first known dictionary**.

Written in **Sumerian and Eblaite**, the tablet paired words from both languages in a kind of **bilingual glossary**, helping scribes learn and translate vocabulary across cultures. This discovery proves that language learning—and even structured linguistic study—was already a thing **4,500 years ago**.

Ebla wasn't just trading goods—it was trading **knowledge**, and doing it with stunning sophistication.

Long before Google Translate, the Eblaites were already **building the bridge between worlds.**

Mind-Blowing Ancient Civilization #53

THE SCYTHIANS TATTOOED THEIR DEAD

The **Scythians**, fierce nomadic warriors of the Eurasian steppe, weren't just known for their archery and horseback skills—they were also early adopters of **tattoo culture.**

When archaeologists unearthed Scythian mummies from the frozen tombs of **Siberia's Altai Mountains**, they were stunned to find **elaborate tattoos** still visible on the preserved skin—some over **2,500 years old.**

These weren't random marks—they depicted **mythical beasts, deer, and battle scenes**, possibly symbolizing status, identity, or protection in the afterlife.

The Scythians didn't just ink themselves for life—they **took their tattoos to the grave.**

Mind-Blowing Ancient Civilization #54

THE MUISCA USED GOLD FOR RITUALS, NOT WEALTH

High in the Andes of present-day Colombia, the **Muisca civilization** didn't just possess gold—they **redefined its meaning**.

Unlike other cultures that hoarded gold as treasure, the Muisca used it in **spiritual ceremonies**, most famously in the **El Dorado ritual**. A Muisca chief would cover himself in gold dust and sail to the center of **Lake Guatavita**, where he'd **offer gold artifacts to the gods** by tossing them into the water.

To the Muisca, gold wasn't currency—it was **a sacred bridge between worlds**.

This ritual helped spark centuries of obsession by Spanish conquistadors, who never found the mythical city—but the **Muisca were never trying to build one**.

Mind-Blowing Ancient Civilization #55

THE MYCENAEANS HAD BOOBY-TRAPPED TOMBS

The **Mycenaeans**—the warrior kings of Bronze Age Greece—weren't just building grand tombs for themselves. They were **rigging them against grave robbers**.

Archaeologists have discovered that some **tholos tombs** (beehive-shaped burial chambers) included **hidden stone slabs** and **false walls**, designed to mislead or crush intruders trying to plunder royal graves.

One tomb near **Argolis** even had a **swinging trapdoor** mechanism that could have sealed shut once entered—an early example of ancient **security tech** mixed with a heavy dose of paranoia.

Forget cursed mummies—these guys were using **actual booby traps** to guard their golden afterlives.

Mind-Blowing Ancient Civilization #56

THE AINU HAD A HIDDEN ISLAND CULTURE

In the far north of Japan, the **Ainu people** developed a distinct civilization that thrived for centuries—**separate from the Japanese mainland culture** we usually read about.

The Ainu lived primarily on **Hokkaido and nearby islands**, building thatched homes, worshipping natural spirits called **kamuy**, and crafting intricate **textiles, tools, and tattoos**. They hunted with poison-tipped arrows and fished with specialized traps, adapting brilliantly to a rugged environment.

Their language is a **linguistic isolate**, unrelated to Japanese or any known language family, and much of their oral tradition was passed down through **epic storytelling and song**.

Though long marginalized, the Ainu are now recognized as **an indigenous people with a rich, ancient legacy**—one that history nearly forgot.

Mind-Blowing Ancient Civilization #57

THE ELAMITES PRECEDED THE PERSIAN EMPIRE

Before Persia rose to dominate the ancient world, the region was home to a powerful and mysterious civilization: the **Elamites**.

Centered in what is now **southwestern Iran**, the **Elamite civilization** dates back over **4,000 years**, with its own writing system, architecture, and royal traditions. Their capital, **Susa**, would later become a key city of the Persian Empire—but it was the Elamites who built it first.

They were rivals of Babylon, allies of the Hittites, and occasionally conquerors of Mesopotamia—yet they remain largely overlooked today.

Their language, **Elamite**, is still undeciphered, and much of their culture remains a puzzle. But they laid the groundwork for what would become one of history's greatest empires.

Mind-Blowing Ancient Civilization #58

THE DACIANS FOUGHT WITH CURVED SWORDS

The **Dacians**, fierce mountain warriors from what is now **Romania**, were such a threat to Rome that Emperor **Trajan** launched two full-scale campaigns just to conquer them.

One of their most distinctive weapons was the **falx**—a terrifying **curved blade** that could **slice through armor and shields** with brutal efficiency. It was so effective that, during the Dacian Wars, Roman soldiers had to **reinforce their helmets and arms** just to survive encounters with it.

The Dacians were eventually defeated, but not forgotten—**Trajan's Column in Rome** still depicts their battles in vivid detail, complete with those menacing blades.

They weren't just rebels—they were a warrior culture that made even Rome rethink its gear.

Mind-Blowing Ancient Civilization #59

THE HITTITES HAD AN ANCIENT PEACE CORPS

The **Hittites**, powerful rivals of Egypt and masters of Anatolia, weren't just about war—they had a remarkable system for **rebuilding and reintegrating conquered regions**.

After taking a city, the Hittites often **restored local rulers**, **rebuilt infrastructure**, and provided legal protections for the population—sometimes even **forbidding looting**. They signed treaties that included **mutual defense clauses**, offered **asylum to refugees**, and kept diplomatic correspondence that reads more like **modern politics than ancient empire-building**.

Clay tablets reveal they were just as concerned with **governance, diplomacy, and justice** as with swords and chariots.

Far from being just conquerors, the Hittites ran an empire with a **surprising sense of order and restraint**.

Mind-Blowing Ancient Civilization #60

THE SILLA KINGDOM USED GOLD-COVERED CROWNS

In ancient Korea, the **Silla Kingdom** (57 BCE – 935 CE) produced some of the most **extravagant royal crowns** the world had never seen — until archaeologists unearthed them in the 20th century.

Made of **pure gold**, adorned with **jade beads**, and decorated with **antler-like spikes**, these crowns weren't just headgear — they were symbols of divine kingship, believed to connect rulers with heaven and nature.

What's even more impressive? They date from the **5th and 6th centuries CE**, showing that Silla royalty had an artistic style and metallurgical skill that rivaled anything happening in Europe at the time.

Hidden in royal tombs for over a thousand years, they remind us that ancient Korea was **a powerhouse of beauty, belief, and brilliance**.

Mind-Blowing Ancient Civilization #61

THE NOK MADE TERRACOTTA BEFORE ROME DID

In what is now **Nigeria**, the **Nok civilization** was creating **terracotta sculptures** as early as **1500 BCE**—centuries before classical Greece and Rome developed their iconic styles.

These sculptures, often life-sized heads with expressive features and elaborate hairstyles, are some of the **earliest known examples of figurative art in sub-Saharan Africa**. They likely served religious or ceremonial purposes, though much about the Nok remains a mystery.

Their artistry, detail, and scale stunned archaeologists when they were first unearthed in the 20th century—and forced a rewrite of assumptions about ancient African art and sophistication.

Long before the Parthenon or the Colosseum, the Nok were already **shaping human expression out of clay**.

Mind-Blowing Ancient Civilization #62

THE ACHAEMENIDS BUILT A POSTAL SYSTEM

Long before Pony Express or FedEx, the **Achae-menid Empire** (Persian Empire) created one of the world's **first organized postal systems**—designed to move royal messages across an empire stretching from **India to Greece.**

Known as the **Angarium**, it relied on **relay stations** with fresh horses and riders stationed along a vast network of roads, especially the famed **Royal Road**, which stretched over **1,600 miles.**

Messages could travel incredible distances in a matter of **days,** thanks to this early express system—so reliable that even **Herodotus**, the Greek historian, praised it.

Sound familiar? The motto of the modern U.S. Postal Service—*"Neither snow nor rain…"*—is based on a description of these **ancient Persian couriers.**

Mind-Blowing Ancient Civilization #63

THE CARTHAGINIANS MASTERED NAVAL TECH

The **Carthaginians**, rivals of Rome and legends of the sea, weren't just brilliant traders—they were **naval innovators**.

Their shipyards could mass-produce **war galleys** using standardized, pre-cut parts—an ancient assembly line that let them build fleets **faster than any other Mediterranean power**. They even pioneered the use of the **corvus**, a boarding device that turned sea battles into hand-to-hand brawls— leveling the playing field against more experienced Roman crews.

Carthage also trained its sailors in advanced **navigation and coastal mapping**, enabling them to explore as far as **West Africa** and possibly even the **British Isles**.

They didn't just sail—they **engineered domination on water**.

Mind-Blowing Ancient Civilization #64

THE SARMATIANS INSPIRED ARTHURIAN LEGENDS

The **Sarmatians**, fierce nomadic horsemen from the **Eurasian steppe**, were such skilled cavalry that the Roman Empire recruited thousands of them into military service.

One Sarmatian unit—**5,500 strong**—was stationed in **Britain** during the 2nd century CE, near Hadrian's Wall. These warriors brought with them **dragon banners, sword rituals**, and tales of warrior leaders who wielded magical weapons.

Some historians believe their traditions **influenced the legends of King Arthur**, especially the imagery of the **knight with the sword**, the **dragon standard**, and a **mythic leader from the East**.

They didn't just fight Rome—they may have helped **shape the mythic DNA of medieval Europe**.

Mind-Blowing Ancient Civilization #65

THE ETRUSCANS USED MIRRORS FOR MAGIC

To the **Etruscans**, mirrors weren't just for vanity—they were **portals to the divine**.

These ancient Italians, who flourished before Rome rose to power, crafted stunning bronze mirrors etched with **mythological scenes, inscriptions**, and images of gods. But more than art, they were used in **rituals, divination**, and even **funerary practices**.

Etruscan priests believed mirrors could **reveal the will of the gods** or glimpse the afterlife. Some were buried with the dead to help guide them in the next world.

For the Etruscans, reflection wasn't about looking at yourself—it was about **looking beyond**.

Mind-Blowing Ancient Civilization #66

THE HARAPPANS HAD TOOTHBRUSHES

The **Indus Valley Civilization** wasn't just ahead in city planning—they were also early adopters of **dental hygiene**.

Archaeologists have found evidence that **Harappans used twigs** from trees like **neem and babool** as natural toothbrushes. These twigs contain **antibacterial properties** and are still used today in parts of South Asia as a traditional method of oral care.

Even more surprising? Some **human remains from Harappan sites** show signs of **dental drilling**—performed with a bow drill—dating back nearly **9,000 years**. It may have been used to relieve tooth pain or infections.

While the rest of the world was gritting its teeth, the Harappans were already **brushing and drilling with precision**.

Mind-Blowing Ancient Civilization #67

THE MELIANS HAD THEIR OWN MICRO-STATE

Tiny but mighty, the ancient island of **Melos (or Milos)** in the Aegean Sea once held its own as an **independent micro-state** during the height of Greek city-state rivalry.

Though small, the **Melians minted their own coins**, maintained a navy, and practiced their own unique blend of **Dorian Greek culture**. They tried to stay neutral during the **Peloponnesian War**, but when they refused to side with Athens, they paid a tragic price.

In 416 BCE, Athens **invaded, executed the men, and enslaved the women and children**—a moment so infamous it became a core case study in power politics.

Thucydides recorded it in the **Melian Dialogue**, a chilling lesson in realpolitik that still echoes in international relations today.

Mind-Blowing Ancient Civilization #68

THE HMONG PRESERVED HISTORY IN CLOTH

The **Hmong people**, an ancient ethnic group from the mountainous regions of **China, Vietnam, Laos, and Thailand**, didn't use writing to record their history—they used **thread.**

Through a traditional art form called **paj ntaub** (pronounced "pan dow"), Hmong women wove **intricate story cloths** that captured genealogies, folklore, migrations, and even battles. These embroidered panels served as **visual records**, passed down through generations.

When the Hmong were displaced during the 20th century, many families brought only these cloths—**portable libraries** of cultural memory stitched into fabric.

Before written scripts or stone tablets, they preserved identity and history with **needle, color, and memory.**

Mind-Blowing
Ancient Civilization
#69

THE TARTESSIANS MINED LIKE MASTERS

The **Tartessians**, a mysterious civilization from ancient **southern Spain**, flourished around **1000 BCE** and may have been one of Europe's **first true urban cultures**.

They built their wealth on the **massive mineral deposits** of the Iberian Peninsula, especially **copper, silver, and gold**. Greek and Phoenician traders sailed west just to access Tartessos's legendary riches—some even believed it was the inspiration for **Atlantis**.

Though their writing remains undeciphered, Tartessian ruins show signs of **urban planning, metallurgy**, and **international trade**—with influences from both **eastern Mediterranean cultures** and indigenous Iberian traditions.

They were Europe's ancient gold rush before anyone knew what a gold rush was.

Mind-Blowing Ancient Civilization #70

THE BANPO USED HEATED FLOORS

At the ancient **Banpo Village** in China, dating back over **6,000 years**, the Neolithic inhabitants developed a surprisingly cozy innovation—**underfloor heating.**

Archaeological evidence shows they used a system known as **"kang"**, where heat from a fire flowed through **hollowed-out spaces beneath clay floors**, warming living spaces during harsh winters.

This early **radiant heating system** predates Roman hypocausts by millennia and proves that even in pre-dynastic times, the Banpo people weren't just surviving—they were **engineering comfort**.

In short, they were living warm, smart, and stylish—**thousands of years before thermostats.**

Mind-Blowing Ancient Civilization #71

THE AVARS USED SIGNAL TOWERS TO COMMUNICATE

The **Avar Khaganate**, a powerful steppe empire in Central and Eastern Europe (6th–9th centuries CE), didn't just conquer—they **coordinated** with remarkable speed.

One of their secrets? A network of **signal towers** and **hilltop stations** used to send **visual messages**—likely using smoke by day and fire by night—across vast distances.

This allowed the Avars to **mobilize troops, monitor borders**, and maintain control over their widespread territory—long before mail couriers or telegraph lines existed.

Their rivals feared their speed, but few realized the Avars had created an **ancient version of long-distance wireless communication.**

Mind-Blowing Ancient Civilization #72

THE MITANNI TAUGHT THE HITTITES HORSE POWER

The **Mitanni**, a powerful but often overlooked kingdom in northern Mesopotamia, were the **original horse lords** of the ancient Near East—and they changed warfare forever.

Their mastery of **horse training and chariot warfare** was so respected that even the mighty **Hittites** learned from them. A surviving Mitanni text—essentially a **horse-training manual**—describes techniques for conditioning, feeding, and handling horses for speed and stamina.

This knowledge spread across empires and helped **transform the chariot into the ancient tank**—a mobile, high-speed weapon platform that dominated battlefields for centuries.

The Mitanni didn't just ride horses—they **rewrote the playbook for ancient mobility and military strategy.**

Mind-Blowing Ancient Civilization #73

THE CHAVIN USED SOUND TO CONTROL CROWDS

Deep in the Andes, the ancient **Chavín civilization** (circa 900 BCE) built ceremonial temples with a shocking feature: **acoustic engineering**.

Inside the **Chavín de Huántar temple**, a maze of stone corridors was designed to **amplify and distort sound**—especially the blasts of **conch shell trumpets**. These eerie, echoing tones could disorient worshippers, enhancing the power of religious rituals and creating an almost **hallucinatory experience**—especially in the presence of psychoactive substances.

Some scholars believe this was intentional: an ancient method of **psychological control** through architecture and sound.

The Chavín didn't just build temples—they **turned their sacred spaces into immersive sound chambers**.

Mind-Blowing Ancient Civilization #74

THE CELTS BUILT HILLFORTS IN RINGS

Long before medieval castles dotted Europe, the ancient Celts built **ringforts**—circular, fortified settlements that blended practicality, defense, and social organization.

These **hilltop enclosures** featured **concentric earthworks, timber palisades**, and sometimes even **stone walls**, with homes and livestock inside. They weren't just military bases—they were **living communities**, often occupied for centuries.

Some, like **Emain Macha in Ireland**, were not only political centers but **sacred sites tied to mythology and kingship**. Many still dot the landscape today, hidden under grassy hills and farmland.

The Celts didn't just defend their world—they **designed it in circles of power, story, and survival.**

Mind-Blowing Ancient Civilization #75

THE AINU HAD BEAR SACRIFICE CEREMONIES

The **Ainu people** of ancient Japan and Sakhalin held one of the most **extraordinary rituals** in human history: the **iyomante**, or **bear sending-off ceremony**.

After raising a bear cub in the village as a guest of honor—**not a pet, but a sacred being**—the Ainu would eventually sacrifice it in an elaborate ceremony believed to **send its spirit to the divine realm**. The bear, considered a **messenger of the gods**, was treated with reverence throughout the process.

This ceremony wasn't about cruelty—it was a **spiritual dialogue** between the human and animal worlds, rooted in deep respect and cosmology.

The Ainu didn't just coexist with nature—they **wove it into their sacred narrative.**

Mind-Blowing Ancient Civilization #76

THE PHILISTINES BREWED BEER LIKE PROS

The **Philistines**, often remembered as biblical villains, were actually skilled artisans, traders—and **craft brewers.**

Archaeologists have uncovered **beer-making facilities** at Philistine sites like **Gath and Ashkelon**, complete with **fermentation vats, grain storage pits, and pottery** designed for drinking and storing brew. They likely adopted and refined techniques from **Egyptian and Levantine neighbors**, producing beer as both a **daily staple and a ritual offering**.

Residue analysis shows traces of **barley-based beer**, sometimes flavored with herbs—centuries before hops became a thing.

So next time you hear about Goliath, remember: the Philistines weren't just warriors—they were **ancient masters of the pint.**

Mind-Blowing Ancient Civilization #77

THE SOGDIANS HAD SILK ROAD HOTELS

The **Sogdians**, legendary merchants of Central Asia, didn't just dominate Silk Road trade—they helped make it **comfortable**.

Scattered across desert routes from **Samarkand to China**, the Sogdians established **caravanserais**—walled inns where merchants and their animals could **rest, eat, trade**, and swap stories. These early **roadside hotels** offered protection from bandits, a place to resupply, and a hub for **multicultural exchange**.

They were more than motels—they were **networking centers**, where deals were struck, news traveled, and cultures collided.

The Sogdians didn't just connect worlds—they **made the road feel like home**.

Mind-Blowing Ancient Civilization #78

THE LIGURIANS DEFIED ROME FOR CENTURIES

The **Ligurians**, an ancient people from the rugged mountains of **northwestern Italy**, were so fiercely independent that even **Rome struggled to subdue them.**

For centuries, they resisted Roman expansion with **guerrilla tactics**, using their knowledge of the terrain to hold off legions that easily steamrolled other regions. Roman generals described them as **"wild and unconquerable,"** and it took repeated campaigns—and forced resettlements—before Rome finally brought them under control.

But even then, Ligurian traditions, languages, and resistance **echoed through the empire's borders**.

They didn't build empires—but they proved that a **small, stubborn culture could hold its ground** against the mightiest power of the ancient world.

Mind-Blowing Ancient Civilization #79

THE PARACAS PRACTICED SKULL ELONGATION

The **Paracas culture** of ancient Peru, thriving from around **800 BCE to 100 BCE**, is known for something truly head-turning—**cranial modification.**

Paracas elites practiced **skull elongation** by tightly binding infants' heads with cloth or boards, gradually shaping them into **tall, conical forms**. This wasn't random—it was likely a marker of **status, identity, or spiritual significance**.

But here's the twist: elongated skulls have been found buried in **lavishly decorated tombs**, alongside fine textiles and jewelry, suggesting these individuals were **powerful or revered**.

To the Paracas, a shaped skull wasn't a deformity—it was a **crown of distinction**.

Mind-Blowing Ancient Civilization #80

THE SABEANS BUILT TEMPLES TO THE MOON

In what is now **Yemen**, the ancient **Sabean civilization** (circa 1200 BCE–275 CE) flourished in the arid heart of Arabia—thanks to trade, engineering, and **devotion to the moon.**

Their primary deity was **Almaqah**, a **moon god**, and they built elaborate temples in his honor—complete with **massive stone pillars**, intricate inscriptions, and astronomical alignments. The most famous, the **Mahram Bilqis** (Temple of the Moon God), was a pilgrimage site for centuries.

The Sabeans also engineered advanced **irrigation systems**, turning deserts into orchards and helping power a kingdom that became a key player in **spice and incense trade** with the Roman and Persian worlds.

Before Mecca rose, the moon ruled in Saba.

Mind-Blowing Ancient Civilization #81

THE TOLTECS INFLUENCED THE AZTEC GODS

Before the rise of the Aztec Empire, the **Toltecs** ruled central Mexico—and their legacy ran so deep that the Aztecs considered them **divine ancestors.**

Centered at **Tula**, the Toltecs built massive pyramids, ball courts, and the iconic **Atlantean warrior statues**, towering stone figures that once supported a temple roof. But their influence went beyond architecture—they passed down **gods, myths, and rituals** that the Aztecs later absorbed.

One major handoff? The god **Quetzalcoatl**—the feathered serpent—who became a central figure in Aztec religion but was **worshipped by the Toltecs first.**

To the Aztecs, the Toltecs weren't just history—they were the **blueprint for civilization.**

Mind-Blowing Ancient Civilization #82

THE ILLYRIANS HAD PIRATE KINGDOMS

The **Illyrians**, ancient tribes from the western Balkans, weren't just warriors—they were **some of the most feared pirates** of the classical world.

Controlling the eastern Adriatic coast, Illyrian fleets raided Roman and Greek merchant ships with such intensity that **Rome launched full-scale naval campaigns** just to stop them. Queen **Teuta**, one of their most notorious leaders, openly supported piracy as **state policy** in the 3rd century BCE.

These weren't rogue bands—they were **state-sponsored sea raiders**, operating from fortified coastal strongholds and thriving off plunder and tribute.

The Illyrians didn't just challenge empires—they **forced Rome to build a navy just to deal with them.**

Mind-Blowing Ancient Civilization #83

THE ZAPOTECS HAD A TOMB WRITING SYSTEM

While the Maya get most of the credit for Mesoamerican writing, the **Zapotecs** were quietly carving out their own script — **centuries earlier.**

At sites like **Monte Albán**, archaeologists have found **stone tombs inscribed with glyphs**, believed to represent names, titles, and possibly even **dates of death**. These carvings may be part of one of the **earliest known writing systems in the Americas**, dating back to around **500 BCE**.

What's wild? Some symbols appear consistently across multiple tombs — suggesting not just decoration, but a **structured system of written language** tied to governance, religion, and ancestry.

Before the codices, before the pyramids of Palenque — **the Zapotecs were already writing the story of the dead.**

Mind-Blowing Ancient Civilization #84

THE OLMECS PLAYED BALL WITH RUBBER

The **Olmecs**, often called the **"mother culture" of Mesoamerica**, didn't just build colossal heads—they also **invented rubber balls** for one of the **oldest team sports in the world.**

Using latex from rubber trees and mixing it with juice from morning glory vines, the Olmecs created a **bouncy, durable material** thousands of years before vulcanization. They used it to play the **Mesoamerican ballgame**, a ritual sport that could involve **ceremony, politics, and even human sacrifice.**

Courts for the game have been found at several Olmec sites, showing that this wasn't just a pastime—it was **a sacred event woven into their worldview.**

Long before basketball or soccer, the Olmecs were already **making plays with science and spirit.**

Mind-Blowing Ancient Civilization #85

THE HATTIANS WORSHIPPED WEATHER GODS

Before the Hittites ruled Anatolia, the land was home to the **Hattians**—a mysterious, pre-Indo-European people who laid the **spiritual foundation** for the civilizations that followed.

The Hattians revered **weather gods**, especially **Taru**, the storm deity who wielded thunder and controlled rainfall—crucial for agriculture. Their mythology and rituals were so influential that the later Hittites **adopted and adapted** many Hattian gods into their own pantheon.

Even the Hittite capital, **Hattusa**, took its name from the earlier Hattian city.

Though their language and culture were eventually absorbed, the Hattians left behind **a stormy spiritual legacy** that echoed through centuries of Anatolian religion.

Mind-Blowing Ancient Civilization #86

THE CHIMÚ BUILT WITH MUD ON A MASSIVE SCALE

Before the rise of the Inca, the **Chimú civilization** ruled the northern coast of Peru—and built one of the **largest adobe cities in the world**: **Chan Chan**.

Covering nearly **eight square miles**, Chan Chan was constructed entirely out of **sun-dried mud bricks**, with intricately carved walls, ceremonial plazas, and royal compounds. At its peak in the 15th century, it may have housed **over 60,000 people**.

The city was laid out with **engineered precision**, including water reservoirs and a **sophisticated canal system** to manage the harsh desert climate.

In a land with no stone, the Chimú created a capital **out of earth—and made it last.**

Mind-Blowing Ancient Civilization #87

THE THRACIANS BURIED KINGS IN GOLD MASKS

The **Thracians**, fierce warriors and skilled artisans of ancient Southeastern Europe, honored their rulers with **lavish burial rituals**—including **golden death masks**.

In tombs across **modern-day Bulgaria**, archaeologists have discovered royal graves filled with **gold jewelry, chariots, weapons,** and intricately crafted masks placed over the faces of the deceased. These masks weren't just decoration—they were believed to help **guide the soul into the afterlife**.

One of the most famous finds, the **Mask of Teres**, rivals anything from Mycenae or Egypt in artistry and opulence.

The Greeks feared them, the Romans fought them—but the Thracians buried their dead like **gods among warriors**.

Mind-Blowing Ancient Civilization #88

THE GUANCHES MUMMIFIED THEIR DEAD

Long before Europeans arrived, the **Guanches**—the indigenous people of the **Canary Islands**—developed a remarkably advanced culture in total isolation, including the practice of **mummification.**

Using techniques similar in some ways to ancient Egypt, the Guanches **carefully wrapped and preserved bodies** with animal skins, resin, and plant materials, then placed them in **caves high in the cliffs**, safe from moisture and scavengers.

Some mummies are so well-preserved that **facial features, hair, and tattoos** are still visible today—despite being over **1,000 years old.**

Cut off from mainland civilizations, the Guanches created **a funerary tradition all their own—hidden in the mountains, and nearly lost to time.**

Mind-Blowing Ancient Civilization #89

THE NABATAEANS MASTERED DESERT PLUMBING

The **Nabataeans**, best known for carving the city of **Petra** into rose-red cliffs, didn't just create architectural wonders—they **engineered the desert.**

Living in one of the driest regions on Earth, they built an incredibly advanced system of **cisterns, aqueducts, and underground channels** to collect and store rainwater. Some of these systems could hold **millions of liters**, ensuring survival for their cities, farms, and trade routes.

They even used **ceramic pipes and pressure regulators**, making them pioneers in **hydraulic engineering** long before modern plumbing.

While others saw desert, the Nabataeans saw **opportunity flowing beneath the sand.**

Mind-Blowing Ancient Civilization #90

THE CUCUTENI BUILT HOMES, THEN BURNED THEM

The **Cucuteni-Trypillia culture**, which thrived in Eastern Europe between **4800 and 3000 BCE**, built sprawling settlements with **hundreds of clay homes**—some of the largest Neolithic communities in the world.

But here's the twist: every few generations, they would **deliberately burn their entire village** to the ground—then rebuild it right on top of the ruins.

Archaeologists still debate the reason. Was it ritual? Sanitation? A symbolic renewal of life? Whatever the cause, this practice created **massive archaeological layers**, giving us a detailed timeline of their evolving society.

For the Cucuteni, destruction wasn't an end— it was **a planned rebirth**.

Mind-Blowing Ancient Civilization #91

THE HIMYARITES BUILT SKYSCRAPER CITIES

In ancient Yemen, the **Himyarite Kingdom** (110 BCE – 525 CE) ruled a desert empire—and constructed cities that rose **vertically**, centuries before the world's great metropolises.

In places like **Shibam**, often called the "**Manhattan of the Desert**," the Himyarites built **multi-story mudbrick towers**, some up to **7 stories tall**, to maximize space and catch cooler air. These weren't just homes—they were **fortresses**, **markets**, and **status symbols**, rising against the harsh desert backdrop.

Protected by walls and designed for efficiency, these early skyscrapers represent one of the oldest examples of **high-rise urban planning** on Earth.

Long before steel and glass, the Himyarites reached for the sky with **nothing but mud and genius.**

Mind-Blowing Ancient Civilization #92

THE SARMATIANS USED SCALE ARMOR

The **Sarmatians**, fierce nomadic warriors from the steppes north of the Black Sea, didn't just fight hard—they fought smart, wearing **highly effective scale armor** made of **metal, horn, or leather plates** sewn onto fabric.

This flexible yet protective armor gave Sarmatian cavalry a major advantage, especially in **hit-and-run tactics** and **close combat**. Roman sources admired—and feared—their gear so much that parts of it were **adopted by Roman cavalry units**.

Their warriors were also among the few in the ancient world known to field **female fighters**, armored and battle-ready.

The Sarmatians didn't just clash with empires—they **suited up for survival and success.**

Mind-Blowing Ancient Civilization #93

THE MANDAEANS REVERE JOHN THE BAPTIST

The **Mandaeans**, a small but ancient religious group from **southern Mesopotamia**, trace their spiritual roots back over **2,000 years**—and their central prophet isn't who you might expect.

While Christianity reveres **John the Baptist** as a forerunner to Jesus, the Mandaeans consider **John as their main prophet**—and reject Jesus altogether. Their rituals focus heavily on **purity, water, and baptism**, which they've practiced **continuously since antiquity**.

They've preserved **sacred texts written in their own language**, Mandaic, a dialect of Aramaic, and their religious practices remain some of the **oldest surviving in the world**.

The Mandaeans are a living link to **ancient Gnostic traditions**—and a faith that has **flowed quietly alongside rivers of history**.

Mind-Blowing Ancient Civilization #94

THE GARAMANTES BUILT UNDERGROUND HIGHWAYS

In the scorching sands of the **Sahara**, the **Garamantes**—an ancient Berber civilization—thrived in what seems like an impossible place.

From around **500 BCE**, they built a network of **subterranean tunnels** called **foggaras**, used to tap deep aquifers and deliver water to surface farms and settlements. But here's the kicker: they also constructed **underground roads** alongside these channels—**cool, shaded passageways** for foot traffic and carts to move goods safely beneath the desert heat.

This innovation helped them maintain a **trade empire**, linking sub-Saharan Africa with Mediterranean markets, long before camel caravans dominated the scene.

Beneath the desert, the Garamantes carved a **cool, connected civilization.**

Mind-Blowing Ancient Civilization #95

THE BACTRIANS MINTED BILINGUAL COINS

In the crossroads of ancient Central Asia, the **Greco-Bactrian Kingdom** fused **Hellenistic and Eastern cultures** like few others—and their coins told the story.

After Alexander the Great's campaigns, Greek settlers ruled over Bactria (modern Afghanistan and Uzbekistan), blending Greek and local influences. Their rulers minted coins with **Greek inscriptions on one side** and **Kharosthi script on the other**, appealing to both **Greek elites and native populations.**

Some coins even featured **Indian deities and Buddhist symbols**, showing just how far their multicultural reach extended.

They didn't just spend money—they used it to **unite worlds through silver and language.**

Mind-Blowing Ancient Civilization #96

THE AKSUMITES USED OBELISKS AS TOMB MARKERS

In the highlands of **ancient Ethiopia**, the **Aksumite Kingdom** (c. 100–940 CE) built towering **granite obelisks**, not for temples or gods—but as **monumental tomb markers**.

These obelisks, some reaching **over 75 feet tall**, were carved from single stones and decorated with **false doors and windows**, mimicking multi-story palaces. They marked the graves of kings and nobles, symbolizing both **power and eternal residence**.

One of the tallest—**the Obelisk of Axum**— was so striking that it was **taken to Italy in 1937** by Mussolini's regime (it was finally returned in 2005).

The Aksumites didn't just build for the living—they **elevated the dead in stone skyscrapers**.

Mind-Blowing Ancient Civilization #97

THE BERBERS CHARTED THE STARS TO TRAVEL

The **Berbers** of North Africa, one of the oldest enduring cultures on Earth, didn't just survive in the Sahara—they **navigated it like a sea**, using the **stars as their compass.**

Long before compasses or GPS, Berber nomads memorized complex **celestial maps**, guiding their caravans across **trackless dunes and stony plateaus** with astonishing accuracy. They could read the sky like a scroll—knowing when to move, rest, or hide from the sun.

Their deep astronomical knowledge shaped not just travel, but also **mythology, calendars, and agricultural cycles**—a science passed through oral tradition for generations.

In the vast emptiness of the desert, the Berbers found **direction in the stars.**

Mind-Blowing Ancient Civilization #98

THE LUWIANS WROTE IN A LOST SCRIPT

In Bronze Age Anatolia, the **Luwians** developed a language and script so distinct that it remained hidden in plain sight for centuries.

They spoke an **Indo-European language** related to Hittite, but wrote it using **Luwian hieroglyphs**—a system completely different from Egyptian writing. These symbols appeared on **stone monuments, seals, and royal inscriptions**, many of which were only deciphered in the 20th century.

Some scholars believe Luwians played a **key role in the mysterious Sea Peoples invasions**, possibly even leading a post-Hittite revival in western Anatolia.

Though their empire fell, the Luwians left behind **a coded legacy still being unlocked today.**

Mind-Blowing Ancient Civilization #99

THE HUNS USED MOBILE FELT TENTS

The **Huns**, feared horsemen of the steppes, didn't build cities—but they mastered the art of **mobility**, living in **portable felt yurts** that let them move entire communities with the speed of a cavalry charge.

Made from **wooden frames and layers of wool felt**, these tents were **warm, windproof, and collapsible**, perfect for life on the move. They could be disassembled and packed onto carts in hours, allowing the Huns to **strike swiftly, vanish, and regroup** before enemies could react.

These mobile homes weren't just shelter—they were a **strategic advantage** that let the Huns dominate from the borders of China to the gates of Rome.

They didn't build empires—they **rolled with them.**

Mind-Blowing Ancient Civilization #100

THE DRUIDS PASSED KNOWLEDGE ORALLY

The ancient **Druids** of Celtic society were more than priests—they were **philosophers, judges, scientists, and memory masters** who carried entire libraries **in their minds.**

Refusing to write down sacred knowledge, Druids relied on **oral tradition**, committing laws, history, poetry, medicine, and astronomy to memory. Some were said to study for **up to 20 years** before becoming fully trained.

This wasn't ignorance—it was intention. They believed the **spoken word was more powerful** than the written one, and by preserving knowledge orally, they made it **sacred, flexible, and alive**.

Long before books and scrolls, the Druids were **walking encyclopedias cloaked in oak and wisdom.**

CONCLUSION

Congratulations! You've just journeyed through *100 Mind-Blowing Ancient Civilizations* and explored the wild, mysterious, and unforgettable stories that prove the ancient world was anything but boring. From lost cities to groundbreaking inventions, sacred rituals to unexplained wonders, this collection has shown that the past is packed with surprises waiting to be uncovered.

But here's the thing about ancient history—it's far from finished. For every story you've read, there are countless more still buried in the sands, hidden in ruins, or waiting to be decoded in forgotten scripts. Maybe this book has deepened your fascination with ancient cultures, or perhaps it's sparked a brand new curiosity about how much we still don't know. Or maybe it's simply reminded you that the ancient world was every bit as strange, complex, and inventive as our own.

The truth is, history isn't just about what happened—it's about the thrill of discovery. And you don't need a time machine or a passport to explore it. All you need is a curious mind and a sense of adventure.

So as you close this book, don't think of it as the end. Think of it as the first step into a world where pyramids, philosophers, mummies, and moon gods all share the same page—waiting for you to ask, *"What else is out there?"*

Until next time, stay curious, stay bold, and remember: the most mind-blowing stories from history… might still be waiting to be found.

ACKNOWLEDGEMENTS

Creating *100 Mind-Blowing Ancient Civilizations* has been a journey filled with curiosity, research rabbit holes, and more than a few late nights marveling at how strange and brilliant the ancient world really was. While my name might be on the cover, this book wouldn't exist without the inspiration, support, and stories passed down—both through time and through the amazing people around me.

First, a massive thank you to all the historians, archaeologists, researchers, storytellers, and lifelong learners who've dedicated themselves to unearthing the past. Your work brings lost worlds back to life, and this book is a small tribute to the wonders you continue to reveal.

To my family and friends—thank you for tolerating my constant "Did you know...?" interruptions and enthusiastic rants about ancient tunnels, sky gods, and clay tablets. Your patience, encouragement, and general willingness to indulge my obsession made this book possible.

To my readers—you're the real treasure. Whether you came here for the mysteries, the myths, or just to learn something wild and unexpected, this book was made with you in mind. Your curiosity is what keeps history alive, and I'm so grateful you decided to take this journey with me.

And finally, to the ancient world itself—thank you for being so endlessly fascinating. You've left behind just enough clues to spark wonder, but enough mystery to keep us searching. This book is for the dreamers, the diggers, and everyone who believes the past still has secrets worth uncovering.

Here's to forgotten empires, hidden truths, and the stories still buried in the dust.

ABOUT THE AUTHOR

Felix Grayson is a storyteller at heart, driven by an insatiable curiosity for the strange, surprising, and downright mind-blowing moments that history has to offer. With a passion for uncovering the wildest and most unbelievable tales from ancient civilizations, Felix has crafted *100 Mind-Blowing Ancient Civilizations* to entertain, amaze, and spark wonder in readers of all ages.

When he's not diving into dusty texts or following the trail of a long-lost legend, Felix enjoys exploring old ruins, devouring history documentaries, and pondering life's biggest mysteries over a quiet coffee in a sunlit corner. A firm believer in the magic of the past and the power of a good story, Felix invites you to take this journey through lost worlds and ancient secrets—proving that history isn't just something behind us, but something still full of wonder.

www.ingramcontent.com/pod-product-compliance
Lightning Source LLC
Chambersburg PA
CBHW031310120626
46554CB00001BA/357